W9-BYS-527

MY FIRST LOOK

AT WEATHER

SNOW FALLS IN THE WINTER IN MANY PLACES

Snow

NICOLE HELGET

CREATIVE EDUCATION

Published by Creative Education

123 South Broad Street, Mankato, Minnesota 56001

Creative Education is an imprint of The Creative Company

Designed by Rita Marshall

Photographs by Dennis Frates, Ted Kinsman, Tom Myers, Tom Stack & Associates (Eric

Sanford, Spencer Swanger)

Copyright © 2007 Creative Education

Printed in the United States of America

Library of Congress Cataloging-in-Publication Data

Helget, Nicole Lea. Snow / by Nicole Helget.

p. cm. — (My first look at weather)

Includes index.

ISBN-13 : 978-1-58341-451-4

1. Snow—Juvenile literature. I. Title. II. Series.

QC926.37.H45 2006   651.57'84—dc22   2005037234

First edition 9 8 7 6 5 4 3 2 1

Snow

How Snow Forms 6

How Snowflakes Form 8

Snowstorms 12

Fun in the Snow 16

Hands-On: Paper Snowflakes 22

Additional Information 24

How Snow Forms

Snow lands on noses. It slips inside mittens. It crunches under boots. It sticks to make snowballs. It melts to make puddles. But how does snow get to Earth?

Snow forms in the air above Earth. Wind lifts tiny bits of dust and plant parts up into clouds. Water **vapor** in the clouds clings to these tiny bits. If it is very cold, the bits and water vapor freeze to make **ice crystals**.

SNOW CAN MAKE A WINTER WONDERLAND

Millions of ice crystals fly around in the cloud. When one ice crystal bumps into another ice crystal, they join. This makes **snow crystals**. The snow crystals get too big and heavy for the cloud. They fall to Earth.

How Snowflakes Form

Snow crystals get warm and sticky as they fall. They stick to other snow crystals to make snowflakes. Snowflakes sparkle because they have **facets**. Facets are like little mirrors that **reflect** light. This is why

Snow protects some plants and animals from cold winter winds. The snow is like a blanket!

piles of snow seem to be filled with lots of shiny diamonds.

Some snowflakes look like needles. Some look like stars. All snowflakes have six sides. No two snowflakes look exactly alike.

THIS SNOW CONTAINS MILLIONS OF SNOWFLAKES

Snowflakes are usually as big as a crayon tip. But sometimes they grow much bigger. In 1951, snowflakes in England were five inches (12.5 cm) across. That is about the size of a sixth-grader's hand!

SNOWSTORMS

Sometimes snow and strong wind make storms called blizzards. The wind may blow snow and make it hard for people to see or travel. Schools and stores may close. Trucks called snowplows may have to push snow off roads.

A farmer named Wilson Bentley

was the first person to take

pictures of snowflakes.

In the mountains, large amounts of snow may become loose and start to move. As the snow slides down the mountain, it may knock down trees and buildings. This is called an avalanche. Avalanches are scary and can hurt or kill people.

SOME PEOPLE CLIMB SNOWY MOUNTAINS

Fun in the Snow

Most of the time, snow does not harm people if they wear warm clothes to protect their skin. People should bundle into coats, boots, and mittens during snowy weather.

It can be fun to use sleds, skis, snowshoes, or snowmobiles to travel over snow. But even without these things, people can have fun in the snow. To build snow forts,

The snowiest place on
Earth is Mount Baker. This is
a mountain in Washington.

ICE CRYSTALS LIKE THESE MAKE UP SNOWFLAKES

snowmen, and snow angels, all you need are arms and legs!

People in some places have parades and festivals in snowy weather. Minnesota has a winter carnival that lasts a few weeks. All around the world, many people enjoy snow!

THESE GIRLS ARE MAKING A "SNOWBUNNY"

Hands-on: Paper Snowflakes

You do not have to get cold to enjoy snowflakes. Try making your own using paper!

What You Need

Paper	Scissors	Sugar
A pencil	A glue stick	

What You Do

1. Draw a circle in the middle of the paper.
2. Use your scissors to cut out the circle.
3. Fold the circle in half. Then fold the half-circle into thirds.
4. Cut out shapes from all three edges. Unfold the paper.
5. Smear glue on your snowflake and sprinkle it with sugar.

Your snowflake has six sides and sparkles—just like a real snowflake!

EVERY SNOWFLAKE LOOKS DIFFERENT

Index

avalanche 14

blizzards 12, 14

clothes 16

clouds 6, 8

ice crystals 6, 8

mountains 14

playing 16, 20

snow crystals 8

snowflakes 8, 10, 12, 22

Words to Know

facets—sides of a snowflake

ice crystals—tiny drops of water and bits of dust frozen together in clouds

reflect—to bounce back; when you look in a mirror, your face is reflected

snow crystals—two or more ice crystals joined together

vapor—tiny drops of water that rise into the air

Read More

Erlbach, Arlene. *Blizzards*. New York: Children's Press, 1997.

Howell, Will C. *Zoo Flakes ABC*. New York: Walker Publishing Company, 2002.

Martin, Jacqueline Briggs. *Snowflake Bentley*. New York: Houghton Mifflin Company, 1988.

Explore the Web

Building a Snow Fort http://www.creativekidsathome.com/activities/activity_81.shtml

Weather Dude: Snow http://www.wxdude.com/page11.html

Weather Wiz Kids http://www.weatherwizkids.com/